REVELATIONS OF A TOUR CADDIE

Global Publishing Group
Australia • New Zealand • Singapore • America • London

REVELATIONS OF A TOUR CADDIE

What Really Happens When The Balls Fly!

Foreword by Greg Norman

DAVID KIGHT

DISCLAIMER

First Edition 2017

National Library of Australia

Cataloguing-in-Publication entry:

Creator: Kight, David, author.

Title: Revelations of a Tour Caddie : What Really Happens When The Balls Fly! /
David Kight.

ISBN: 9781925288094 (paperback)

Subjects: Caddies--Anecdotes.
Golfers--Anecdotes.
Caddying--Anecdotes.
Golf--Tournaments--Anecdotes.
Golf--Rules.

Published by Global Publishing Group
PO Box 517 Mt Evelyn, Victoria 3796 Australia
Email info@GlobalPublishingGroup.com.au

Printed in China

For further information about orders:
Phone: +61 3 9739 4686 or Fax +61 3 8648 6871

To my father for giving me a love of this great game at a young age and an appreciation of the beauty of a great layout not just hitting a ball.

To my mother for her love, support and understanding of my overseas trip.

To my loving wife for her patience, support and love of my creative projects including this big one!

To my gorgeous girls for their love, laughter and honesty.

To Shady whose big heart and smile was taken from us too early – we miss you Bud!

ACKNOWLEDGEMENTS

It has been an honour and privilege to write this book. As with any major project there are a number of very special people who contributed to making this book happen. So, I'd like to take this opportunity to say "THANK YOU".

Firstly, I'd like to thank all the players in Australia and Europe who have been gracious enough to have me caddie for them. From those members at Metropolitan in Melbourne where I learnt my trade as a teenager to the professionals on the European Tour of 1991.

To Greg Norman for the most amazing day a teenager could have – filming his first golf instructional video and for bestowing on me the great honour of writing the Foreword for this book!

To Paul Daley, a published golf author of many books, who has chatted, supported and encouraged me on the journey to releasing my first book.

To Mike Clayton for looking out for me as a young rookie Aussie on the European Tour of '91 and for his time and advice in the writing of this book.

To Darren Stephens from Global Publishing for delivering me a WOW moment – when he rang me with the news that I was accepted into his author program.

To Kelly and the other awesome staff at Global Publishing for your guidance, support and assistance in getting this finished and published.

To Jon Brenton, Sonia, Belinda for their assistance in helping me achieve my goals.

To Kelli for the final kick in the bum to get through the procrastination and finish this book!

Norman hitting his approach shot to the 1st green at Huntingdale during the Australian Masters in the early 1980's.

1991

Month	Dates	Event	Venue
Feb	21-24	Girona Open	Pals, Girona, Spain
	28-3	Fujitsu Mediterranean Open	L'Esterel Latitudes, St Raphael, France
March	7-10	Open de Baleares	Santa Ponsa, Mallorca
	14-17	Catalan open	Bonmont, Tarragona, Spain
	21-24	Portuguese Open	Estela, Oporto, Portugal
	28-31	Volvo Open di Firenze	Ugolino, Florence, Italy
April	11-14	Jersey Open	La Moye Golf Club, Jersey
	18-21	Benson & Hedges International	St Mellion, Cornwall, UK
	25-28	Madrid Open	Puerta de Hierro, Madrid, Spain
May	2-5	Crédit Lyonnais Cannes Open	Cannes Mougins, France
	9-12	Peugeot Spanish Open	Club de Campo, Madrid, Spain
	16-19	Lancia-Martini Italian Open	Castelconturbia, Nr Milan, Italy
	24-27	Volvo PGA Championship	Wentworth Club, Surrey, UK
	30-2	Dunhill British Masters	Woburn, Bucks, UK
June	6-9	Murphy's Cup	Fulford, York, UK
	13-16	Belgian Open	Royal Waterloo, Brussels, Belgium
	20-23	Carrolls Irish Open	Killarney, Co Kerry, Ireland
	27-30	Peugeot French Open	National Golf Course, Paris, France
July	3-6	Torras Monte Carlo Golf Open	Mont Agel, Monaco, France
	10-13	Bell's Scottish Open	Gleneagles Hotel, Perthshire, UK
	14-14	* Seniors British Open	Royal Lytham & St Annes, UK
	18-21	120th Open Championship	Royal Birkdale, Lancs, UK
	25-28	Heineken Dutch Open	Noordwijk, Nr Leiden, Netherlands
August	1-4	Scandinavian Masters	Drottningholm, Stockholm, Sweden
	8-11	European Pro-Celebrity	TBA Royal Liverpool, Hoylake (handwritten)
	15-18	NM English Open	The Belfry, Nr Birmingham, UK
	22-25	Volvo German Open	Hubbelrath, Düsseldorf, Germany
	29-1	GA European Open	Walton Heath, Surrey, UK
Sept	5-8	European Masters-Swiss Open	Crans-sur-Sierre, Switzerland
	12-15	Trophée Lancôme	St Nom-la-Bretèche, Paris, France
	16-17	* Equity & Law Challenge	Royal Mid-Surrey Golf Club, UK
	19-22	Epson Grand Prix	St Pierre, Chepstow, UK
	27-29	* Ryder Cup	Kiawah Island, S Carolina, USA
	26-29	Austrian Open	Gut Altentann, Salzburg, Austria
Oct	3-6	Mercedes German Masters	Stuttgart, Germany
	10-13	* Dunhill Cup	St Andrews, UK
	10-13	BMW International Open	Munich, Germany
	17-20	* Toyota World Match Play	Wentworth Club, Surrey, UK
	24-27	Volvo Masters	Valderrama, Sotogrande, Spain
	31-3	* World Cup of Golf by Philip Morris	Le Querce, Rome, Italy
Nov	7-10	* Asahi Glass Four Tours Championsh.	Royal Adelaide, Australia
	7-10	* Benson & Hedges Trophy	TBA
Dec	19-22	* Johnnie Walker World Championship	Tryall, Jamaica

* PGA European Tour Approved Special Events

Sanctioned by PGA EUROPEAN TOUR

The 1991 Volvo European Tour Schedule Card.

"Remember life is like a round of golf ... full of ups and downs!"

CONTENTS

FOREWORD

By Greg Norman

I consider myself very fortunate to have made a living doing something I love, which is playing golf. Having spent 331 weeks as the No. 1 player in the world, I know what it takes to win and stay on top. One of the many things that comes into play is the relationship a player has with his caddie.

In golf, caddies are the only people who really understand the players – it is a unique relationship that doesn't exist in any other sport. Tennis players have coaches and race car drivers have pit crews, but no other individualised sport has an 'assistant' who is as vital to the success or failure of the athlete as a caddie to a player during a Tournament.

I have had a few caddies during my playing career, with Steve Williams and Tony Navarro as the two longest-serving. With these caddies, there needed to be a special bond in our relationship to endure the ups and downs of a career at the top for over twenty years. Words can never express what we went through over the years and the thousands of miles we travelled together.

The person on the bag needs to be a mate, psychologist, comedian, listener,

conversationalist, meteorologist and strategic golfer. Caddies devote entire careers to finding the actions and words that will inspire the best from players under pressure.

In 1984 when I made my first golf instructional video at Metropolitan Golf Club, a teenager caddied for me there – patiently carrying my bag and picking up the hundreds of balls I hit to various holes and out of bunkers onto the 7th green. That teenager was David Kight.

In this book, David shares his own caddying experiences along with great stories from other professional caddies. Let *Revelations of a Tour Caddie* be an inside look to what life as a caddie is really like. Armed with this knowledge, you may never look at a caddie the same way again.

Greg Norman

Chapter 1

My Love of Golf / Early Caddying Days

My father playing golf at Sorrento Downs on the Mornington Peninsula near Melbourne.

CHAPTER 1

My Love of Golf / Early Caddying Days

I developed a real love for golf around ten years of age as I had a father who was mad about the game. My dad used to practice swing in the backyard of our suburban home and leave marks (divots) of where he had swung in the grass of our backyard lawn – much to my mother's disgust. He would practice swing there nearly every night to prepare for his weekly Saturday round with his mates at Amstel Golf Club. As he got a bit older he decided to hit into an old car tyre to strengthen his forearms and wrists to help him to continue to drive as far as he used to.

My father had stumbled into golf when a hamstring injury had kept him from

playing Aussie Rules football for VFA team Oakleigh. This twist of fate had given him a love of a game that would last his whole life, even in his 60s – before his early death he would find a plot of grass to hit golf balls. He would take himself to every local park until the Council officers kicked him off, then he would find another patch of land with grass on it and hit balls there.

He got himself to a handicap of three and played junior pennant for Keysborough after what may have seemed like a cruel injury blow in his mind, yet it was something that he obviously created on a certain level. This gave him the opportunity to play and pursue a game that would give him great joy, that he loved and was passionate about how to play it. He really loved the history of the game and its great players – Cotton, Hogan, Locke, Jones, Nicklaus etc.

He became mad about the game and had Henry Cotton books of 'how to swing each club', which he studied over and over till they fell apart. They were in black and white and had frame by frame photos of how to hit every type of club – driver, fairway irons, wedges and sand irons. My father had a great knowledge and understanding of the golf swing but as a rebel, stubborn teenager I refused to listen to his 'swing advice' and our golf games became me down one side of the fairway, my dad down the other and my mother down the middle trying to keep the peace.

Now funnily I don't remember caddying for my father, yet I probably did a few times. He usually went off to play with his mates and I took myself off to my local club to caddie for members where I could make some money and get home easily. Now I loved my dad but maybe it was better that we didn't mix family and a serious sport. I don't remember him saying "Why don't you come and caddie for me today pal?", maybe he wanted some time with the boys as an escape from his hard 8–5 job building roads, dams and bridges as a civil engineer. It's a bit hard to have laughs and swear with the boys if you have your son caddying for you or you might worry about the rude jokes and banter in the Clubhouse at the 19th Hole after some of you have had a few drinks! Looking back now he wouldn't have been able to 'be himself' if he worried about what I might come home and tell our mother.

He gave me such a love of this game that I would go outside every night in summer and putt around the holes I had created in my front and back yard. Using old fruit tins as cups I designed a nine-hole layout in my yard with bunkers and trees to guard the fairways. These nine holes had par 3, 4 and 5s included, and I named it Watership Down Golf Club and listed my friends and family as office bearers – captain, secretary and treasurer, etc. I ran a Tournament for my mates when I was around 14 and we played 18 holes with scorecards I had made.

From this humble beginning, I then created, with my brother, the Cousin's Cup annual golf Tournament which included my male and female cousins and their partners and lasted for ten years or so. Whilst it was a basic Tournament organiser role I had to confirm tee-times and final numbers with the course we would play at, chase certain cousins to confirm who was or wasn't playing and then often pay the total or a deposit to the Club a week before the round.

Well at around 11 or 12 years old, I decided to go down the road (a ten-minute bike ride downhill) to my nearest private golf course in Mt Waverley and ask for a caddie job. This course was Riversdale, which in the 1960s and '70s hosted some major golf tournaments and was where David Graham began his professional career. The Club professional at the time was Peter Speed, who took my name and found me a member who was looking for a caddie. I guess I caddied there for six months or so and then went back to running the boundary line for my brother's local footy team. Riversdale was good and close to my home and the members were nice enough to a young boy who knew something about golf. It was around that time that I got my first set of clubs or at least a new bag and some of dad's old clubs to form a set and started to play with friends at local public courses.

One of my games at that time was a Sunday morning with a few mates from my high school who were better golfers than me and had a real set of clubs. We got to about the 6th hole and I liked to have a bit of a laugh so I decide to do my best Lee Trevino impersonation from Peter Alliss' *Pro Celebrity Golf* which was on television at the time. Now the two guys I was playing with were more serious about their game and score than me. One was Pete who was a conservative dresser and conscientious student at school. The other, Mark, was dressed well and had very nice clubs, but had a bit more of a sense of humour and whilst he studied hard at school, enjoyed a good joke. This particular hole had a steel ladder attached to a telegraph pole to allow you to climb up and see over the blind fairway drive to make sure players were clear of your possible drive.

I stood up there as Mark had the honour and proceeded to ham it up and put on my best Trevino – "That's a good shot there, Ben, you're hitting the ball well today Ben, make sure you don't hook it Ben!!" Now Mark was about to tee off and whilst he started laughing, he told me to shut up so he could concentrate and hit his drive. I made a few more comments then stopped to allow him to stop laughing his head off and hit his tee shot. I made one more quick comment as he was in his backswing and as he came down he miss hit his drive and took a chunk out of his new driver as he hit underneath the ball so much! Man, did I scurry down that ladder quickly as he chased me with the driver and was going to belt me, cos I had caused him to chip his precious, new wooden driver.

In my teenage years as I first took up golf I didn't have lessons just tried to copy my father or pick it up on my own. I suppose I was too stubborn to listen carefully to his tips, which in hindsight could have made me a much better golfer now! Years later I had some lessons with my swing doctor – Victorian Junior team coach, Richard Cooney – who sized me up for clubs, which I then bought from him with great help from Spalding golf representative Spider! Richard gave me a tricky yet handy practice strategy to keep my swing plane straight – stand with your back facing a fence and swing. Now this felt strange for a while, yet I understood his reasoning and it made me concentrate on swinging straight back for fear of hitting the fence!

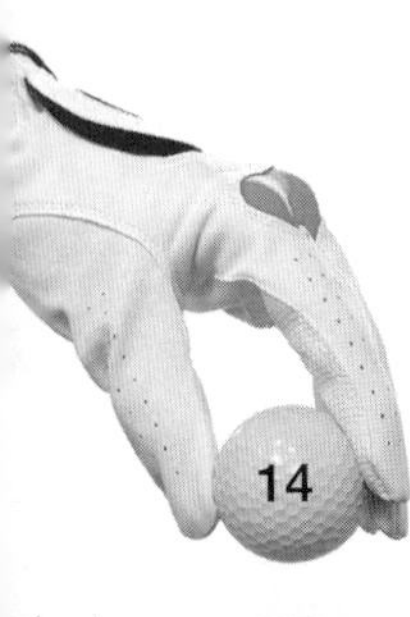

Chapter 2

Live Your Dreams!

Lee Trevino, the drawcard for the 1982 Victorian Open, walks off the 9th green at Metropolitan Golf Club in Melbourne.

CHAPTER 2

Live Your Dreams!

After caddying at Riversdale for a short time I was at school with a kid who lived behind the 2nd green at Metropolitan. Now Micky J didn't like or know much about golf but his house backed onto the 2nd green at Metro and he was good mates with the son of the club professional, who was a character rather than the golf lover; well-spoken person that his dad Brian Twite was. Now Mick and young Twitey hung around with many of the 'tough' boys from Oakleigh and weren't lining up to caddie and say 'Yes sir, No sir' to private course members.

I used to ride my bike over to Metro, as I came to call it, and my route took me past my grandmother's house. So, on the way there or on the way home if it wasn't getting dark, I used to call in and chat to my nana and my great aunty and tell them about how many balls I had found and who I had caddied for. Also, my nana was keen on sport and loved to have a bet on the horses and listen to the Aussie Rules footy, so I would get an update on how she had gone on the punt and who had won the Saturday football games. If it wasn't too dark, I would drop in and get offered a drink or bickie as all nanas would do. Otherwise I would ride along some major roads and then footpaths if it started to get dark at the end of this five-kilometre ride home. The killer was slowly zig-zagging my way up Stanley Avenue which was a 60-degree angled hill not far from my home. After walking 6400 metres-plus for my player sometimes the last thing I needed was a steep hill towards the end of my ride home, yet I was determined not to get off and walk the bike up the remainder of this hill!

Over the years, I caddied for many different members but one stands out due to his unfortunate name as a golfer and my naivety in asking his advice on a medical matter one day. His name was Dr Crapp, and he was a handy, average golfer with an unusual backswing. He was very good to me and he played nearly every week with his good friend Pat Ramsden, who I could tell had been a handy golfer when he was younger.

One Saturday afternoon we are walking down the fairway, when I decided to ask about an injury. I said, "Doctor, just wondering how I can help my ankle that I twisted at footy last week?" He smiled and said, "David I am a dentist not a general practice doctor." Well I felt like I wanted to crawl under the grass of the fairway – I didn't realise that doctor could be any range of physician or specialist, I just thought doctor meant doctor!

As a young boy earning $5 for four hours work you don't think about any 'bigger picture', you just push a buggy for a rich person at an exclusive Club in Melbourne and speak politely and tell them how good a shot it was because that is all you know. If you haven't caddied for a great professional golfer then to you these middle-aged men hit the ball okay or at least appear to 'play to their handicap', so you hand them the club they ask for and give advice only when asked, and hold the flagstick and tell them how unlucky they were when a close putt misses. Even if a cocky teenager really thinks 'Come on old boy I could have made that putt!', that's the comment you would save for another caddie in your group or after the round in the back of the pro shop with the other caddies and guys who worked there. For me at age 12 I didn't know any better, I enjoyed golf and this was a Saturday job for me that whilst not paying as much as working at Coles or Woolworths or McDonald's, still gave me some tangible rewards. I could play 18 holes on Sundays before 9 am and after 4 pm at Metropolitan Golf Club, which was and still is one of the top five courses in Melbourne.

So, I would ask my dad to drop me off and play on my own or with other caddies at 8 am on Sunday mornings, when the curators were still mowing the fairways or watering the greens. In 1978, this was probably worth $40 a round if you had to pay, so being able to play a round at such a private course in the Sandbelt (renowned as one of the greatest stretches of golf courses in the world), was worth more than a better wage or free fries at McDonalds!

Little did I realise then that this course and job would allow me to rub shoulders with some of the best golfers and sportsmen in the world. I was so excited as I carried the bag for my golfer and felt really important as I walked over to my player on the practice fairway. The emotion was strong as one of nerves and absolute joy as I was walking on cloud nine as a kid in my late teens carrying a bag in a professional golf Tournament. It felt like I was famous in my mind as I could walk the fairways with famous professional golfers in our group. I was probably oblivious to whether my player was playing well or was going to make the weekend cut because my heart was racing for just being there – what a thrill this kid from the suburbs caddying in a major golf Tournament shown on national television.

I went from this kid getting a caddie job at the Victorian Open to spending the day with a young Greg Norman as he made his first instructional golf video. In hindsight, I was a kid who the professional asked to collect balls and carry the clubs of this up and coming blond-haired guy from Queensland who was quickly becoming the best golfer in Australia by the Tournaments he had won. As you consider the true reality of this, it becomes apparent that I am one of few Australians who can claim that he ‘caddied for Greg Norman’, even though I really collected the golf balls he hit, cleaned his clubs and raked over the bunkers. At the time, I still had an awareness of who I was caddying for – it was an amazing experience to spend the day with him and to feel absolute joy at having the honour of caddying for him, holding his bag and looking after his clubs.

It was a very basic production team, the producer/cameraman with Norman and me. We ate sandwiches in his car, a Rover and he had a range of golf clubs in the boot. I was this star-struck kid who was in awe of this golfer who was quickly becoming the best in the country and beginning to take on the world. I think I rode my bike the five kilometres home that day with a smile that couldn't be wiped off my face as I had just witnessed one of the greatest sporting days of my life. This is one of those highs when someone could almost do anything to you and you would still be smiling-running on adrenalin of such an amazing experience. Little did I realise then that he would go onto being the No.1 golfer in the world and one of the greatest the game has ever seen!

It's a great story to tell at parties when you find yourself chatting to a keen golfer or just someone who knows and understands sport – you are almost saying Jack Nicklaus in terms of his name being well-known around the world. It's great for the self-esteem and ego when people respond with, "oh man how lucky are you?!" Even though Norman was a great golfer, he also had an aura and charisma about him that meant people knew him like a Pele, Ronaldo, Borg or Tiger. He strode the fairways of Australia in those days as the emerging Great White Shark, he had such a presence with his blond hair, strong body and tall stature.

I also got to stand at the back of the audience in the entrance to the member's locker room who were being enthralled with stories by Lee Trevino the master joke and storyteller. I was that excited little teenager who hung on every word of this hilarious joke- and story-teller. He must have had the crowd laughing their heads off for half an hour or more! Your eyes lit up as he recounted story after story of life on the professional golf tour or caddies and other people he had encountered in his life.

Also, I got the autograph of Seve Ballesteros and the great West Indian cricketer Viv Richards by being in the pro shop when they played or needed clubs fixed by the resident golf professional, Brian Twite. This is about living your dreams – as a teenager I couldn't comprehend this outlook or perspective on 'life', I was just having fun and being in the moment. A boy from Mt Waverley, in the eastern suburbs of Melbourne gets to live this dream life, it's about creating whatever you want in life and going with it. I didn't sit around at home watching television on a Saturday thinking about what might be, I was out there doing something that I loved and getting paid something for it. I subconsciously put myself in the position of being around top golfers and world-renowned sportsmen so I could be in their world and be famous by association. It may have meant a teenager being able to boast or brag to his mates or school friends that he had met Seve Ballesteros or caddied for Sam Torrance or driven Ian Woosnam out to the course one day.

For my life, this job on a Saturday had me at a course where some of the best Australian and overseas golfers played in big Tournaments of the late '70s, early '80s. I got to hang out in the back of the pro shop whilst world famous golfers got their clubs fixed or adjusted by the professional, and just watch and listen to them. Just being in their presence was enough, I was able to go home and tell my best audience – my golf-loving dad – who I had seen, listened to or stood beside. These were all household names and world-famous golfers to my father, so he loved hearing about Trevino telling jokes and stories in the foyer of the men's locker room or Seve getting his 3-iron regripped by the Club professional at the back of the pro Shop where all the club fixing happened.

Had I chosen this for my life? Living a 20-minute bike ride from two golf courses that hosted some of the biggest Tournaments on the Australian Tour –the Australian Open, Australian Masters and the Victorian Open? I don't think this was luck but fate or 'meant to be', I had made a choice on an unconscious level to be surrounded by these great situations or circumstances – a 12-year-old boy who was from a middle-class family in a growing suburb of Melbourne had made a choice on a certain level to have these famous golfers and celebrities around him. Most kids my age in that suburb were playing footy or cricket on Saturday afternoons or running the boundary and getting a few dollars for it. They were happy with that as they loved the game and didn't need anything else exciting in their lives.

Yet I decided that whilst I enjoyed this aspect of life for a sporting teenager in Melbourne, that it was okay to ride my bike for 20 minutes to allow me to be at a golf club that was to host major golf Tournaments and have international stars playing there. It didn't matter that I needed to push the buggy of older, rich members for parts of the year, if this allowed me to fox for balls on the practice fairway or caddie for golfers at the Pro-Am or later in the actual Tournament. There was nothing like walking past the galleries as you went to get more balls for your player to hit on the practice range, or to wet the towel to help clean his clubs properly. You felt like a rockstar as you walked around the putting green, whilst your player practised his putting and you threw his balls back to him. It didn't matter how big or important or young and unknown they were, you had a caddie's bib or overalls on and it felt important to be walking around the practice fairway with galleries of people watching you!

The money was insignificant, as it felt loving to you to be carrying a bag of a professional golfer at a Tournament that was televised around the country or world. It felt good to be able to tell your friends at school that you caddied for someone, regardless of whether they played or understood anything about golf. There was a guy who managed to caddie for David Graham at the Masters at Huntingdale and he was a single-figure handicap golfer from there and he was pretty happy with himself. Apart from his wage he was given a pair of golf shoes which at the time sounded like a good present from a pro who was probably given them for free by his sponsored shoe company, or he was returning to the States and didn't want to have to pack them in his luggage. Those were the sorts of stories that young keen golfers loved to tell and hear about – that they received something special from their player that no one else got – a pair of golf shoes or a dozen new pro golf balls or his old pro golf bag!

Now there is also the not so glamorous side of life as a caddie, when you are living in a caravan and driving yourself to the course in country Victoria. I caddied for a young pro who may have made the cut or weekend, yet it's like the film *Sliding Doors* – you can have two possible outcomes from such a situation or experience. One is that as your player is about to miss the cut, life can feel so flat as you know you won't be 'busy' or involved for the weekend rounds of the Tournament. The cut for a caddie is that fine line between pleasure and pain – miss the weekend, collect your week's pay and go and drown your sorrows at the pub or go home.

In contrast if your player makes the weekend and then starts to play really well on the Saturday you have a swagger about you, a real joy and confidence that means ‘I am going to make some good money and I am feeling great because my player is playing well and I can share his good play and joy at a good result’. Getting to ride his birdie putts home on the green and high-five him or shake his hand for a great putt or hole is a natural adrenalin rush that the sportsmen themselves usually get from great feats or amazing victories!

To be on your own, since you don’t know too many of the other caddies and are too nervous to chat to them about where they are going for dinner or to have a few drinks in a country town isn’t that great. It feels very grounding compared to waltzing around on the putting green at Huntingdale in the Masters, feeling like you are a star regardless of who you are caddying for. But alas that is the life of a caddie, just like a round of golf, it is full of ups and downs, the rough and the putting green!

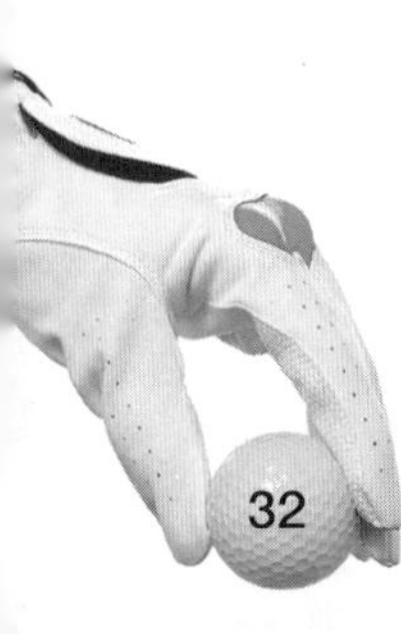

Chapter 3

Caddying in Melbourne – The Australian Tour

A young Greg Norman practices his chip shots at the practice putting green at Metropolitan Golf Club during the 1981 Victorian Open.

CHAPTER 3

Caddying in Melbourne – The Australian Tour

As I mentioned earlier, I started caddying as a 12-year-old at Riversdale Golf Club in Mount Waverley, which was a 20-minute bike ride from my house. I arrived there on a Saturday and asked the club professional, Peter Speed, if anyone needed a caddie. I was hooked up with a member and once I introduced myself we went to tee-off at our first hole.

Riversdale was a bit up hill and down dale as my parents used to say and there were a few steep climbs, which meant caddies were in demand for older members. I think I got a few dollars in 1976 and maybe a soft drink halfway if I was lucky. As a caddie there, I was able to play the course on Sundays, so after a while I would ride down with my clubs on my back and play nine holes.

A few years later I was told by a mate who lived over the back fence from the 2nd green, that the Metropolitan Golf Club in South Oakleigh was a good place to caddie and they needed caddies. He happened to be best mates with the teenager son of the professional Mr Brian Twite, so he said he would put in a good word for me. So, I decided to ride the five-kilometre journey over and try my luck.

Now in terms of the type of members this was different to Riversdale; it was a bit more exclusive with many doctors, lawyers and businessmen from all over Melbourne being members there. As I rode my bike into the car park there were many Mercedes, BMWs and Rolls Royces adorning the rows.

This was the beginning of a real love of golf and a bias to this course that would see me caddie here for over five years. In this time I caddied for many different members including the captain and was introduced by the professional as ‘our best caddie’ to a group of visitors from a country golf course to help get me a bag for the day. It’s great for a 15-year-old to be introduced in such a way and I’m sure my local knowledge helped the player that I caddied for that day.

In 1979, the Australian Open was held there, so I got to caddie for someone in the Pro-Am and worked foxing for balls on the practice fairway during the Tournament. I remember standing beside the assistant professional at around six o’clock on the Friday night and a young blond-haired Greg Norman was arguing about the practice fairway being closed as he wanted to hit balls to work on his swing. We had been told to collect the last balls with the ride on machine and pack up the table and return all the practice balls to the back of the Pro Shop. The very confident young Norman was eager to hit some balls after his round and said to the assistant pro "Come on guys, the days just started" to see if this would convince us to give a him a bucket of balls. The guy stood by his decision and Norman was forced to walk off without hitting any balls. Not sure if he would have said 'No' to him five years later when he was winning Tournaments in Australia and all round the world.

Later, on the Sunday afternoon we were watching the final holes on a little television in the back of the pro shop as Jack Newton was in the clubhouse with a one stroke lead. Norman had left himself a tricky little par putt to tie him and force a play-off. It was a right to left slightly downhill four or five foot putt, which he slid past, and Newton was the 1979 Australian Open champion. After the presentation, I got Newton's and other Australian golfer's autographs on a little pad I had taken along.

In the early 1980s I caddied for a range of young Aussie pros at the Australian Masters at Huntingdale Golf Course. Now my nana had been a member there and I also had mates from school who played there, so I knew the course fairly well.

I also managed to get the bags of some overseas players too, like a young Michael 'Nobby' McLean from England.

Now he had a driving trick in that he used a Ping driver and hit the ball off the deck, that is no tee. He would push up some grass with his club and then sit the ball on top and just hit his driver off it. Now he played some good golf for the unknown young English pro and managed to get himself onto the leader board by Sunday afternoon. Even though I was a young caddie I was sure that my 'local knowledge' had helped him play so well and that I might be slung a tip or bonus for my good work.

When it wasn't forthcoming I rode around to the nearby cheap hotel in Carnegie, a nearby suburb, to see if he wanted to give me something extra. Well of course this was the Monday morning after the Tournament by which time he was probably halfway to London on the first British Airways flight on Sunday night! I did end up caddying beside him on the European Tour but probably decided it was too long ago to remind him but I'm sure I told the story to other English caddies to see what they thought I deserved.

Now the tradition in the '80s when the Masters was the second biggest golf Tournament in Australia after the Australian Open was that some of the overseas players were given courtesy cars for their caddies to drive them around. In 1983–84, when I landed the bag of Sam Torrance, I was assigned one of these to pick him up from the airport and collect him from his hotel each day of the Tournament. So, the Tuesday practice round day I rolled up to the hotel in Albert Park in Melbourne to collect Sam for the day. He wasn't in the hotel lobby so they let me ring his room and he said, "Davy can't practice today I'm too tired see you tomorrow for the Pro-Am." Now I don't know if his excuse was jetlag or he stayed up too late playing snooker, drinking scotch and smoking cigars and couldn't be bothered practising on a course he had never seen or played before.

So, I was just about to drive home when Ian Woosnam and his caddie said are you going to the course? Well I wasn't really but when you have the chance or honour to drive a legend of the game like Woosie then you don't pass up an opportunity like that, so I happily drove them out to the course. On the way we talked about golf, life and what they thought of Australia, and he and his caddie were two of the nicest people you'd ever meet, so I have happily told people over the years that I drove Ian Woosnam out to the course that day.

Anyway, Sam is fine the next day and we play in the Pro-Am and he has a drink with the players from his group then asks me to drive him next door to Metropolitan to the Carbine Club corporate luncheon. So, while he goes in to a free lunch I drop into my old pro shop and chat to the assistant pros out the back while they are cleaning clubs and taking off certain members in *Caddyshack* fashion – this is a club where members ask you to do all sorts of little favours to satisfy their idiosyncrasies and so certain caddies and trainee professionals will show off out the back of the pro shop where their professional can't hear them and impersonate or criticise some of their demands.

Sam plays well this week and we are in contention till the 13th hole on Saturday. When I say we are in contention it is for second place as Greg Norman holds a 7-shot lead as he often did in local Australian Tournaments in his early days. So, Sam hit his drive into the middle of the 13th, a short, narrow par 4 and at this stage we are looking good for a top ten finish.

Then he proceeds to take double bogey there and double bogey on the next hole and as the wheels are falling off I can't say much as a young caddie who doesn't know which approach will work best for him, so I weather the storm and we get to the 18th hole with as little damage as possible. Now mentally I am sure I said all the positives the next day, but Huntingdale can be a harsh course if you aren't straight and I think he shot two or three over and we finished top 30 somewhere. After the round, I manage to get a mate into the clubhouse and we are drinking and chatting up women and having a fine old time as everyone is in a good mood at the end of a Tournament. Knowing I can't drink and drive I am conscious of only having a few light beers until Sam says, "I'll drive back to the hotel Davy, I have an International licence, it doesn't matter if I get pulled over for drink driving."

So, I relaxed and my mate and I were able to have a few drinks then we went into the hotel with Sam for the drive and to make sure the courtesy car got back okay and the not so glamorous end to the story is that we caught the train home from the city and walked home to our houses. A much better ending would have been that we kicked onto a disco and had a few beers with Sam and then played pool with him till the early hours of the morning before we caught a taxi home.

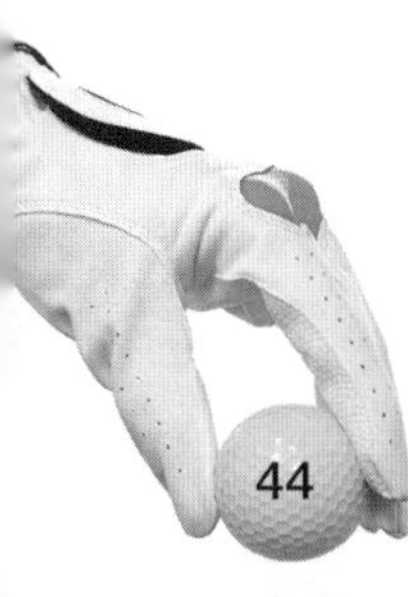

Chapter 4

The Journey – What Are Caddies Really Searching For?

Peter Senior and caddie Carlo walking onto the 9th green during the 1994 Australian Masters at Huntingdale Golf Club in Melbourne.

CHAPTER 4

The Journey – What Are Caddies Really Searching For?

What are caddies around the world searching for – is it the money, fame, success, mateship, lack of security, fear of commitment to a proper relationship, self-esteem, WOW moments, freedom, partying lifestyle, variety of towns/cities/countries/cultures, friendship or just travel? For many of them I believe it is a mixture of some of these, yet if you surveyed a range of professional caddies from the two biggest tours – the European Tour and the US PGA Tour – I'm sure they may have a similar top five.

Do you start caddying because you enjoy golf and it is an easy way to see the world? If you are caddying in Europe, you are almost in a different country every week. Now that the tour has become more global you even get to go to Dubai in the Middle East as part of the extended 'European Tour'. To be honest there is only the top percentage who are caddying for players in the top ten of that tour that can make a 'good wage'. So probably then money is part of their highest five values, whereas a caddie who has a player who is younger, new to the Tour or not finishing in the money regularly then for them 'money' will probably not be in their top five reasons for being a caddie. Perhaps love of the game or that constant hope that their player may finish top ten or win one week is the dangling carrot that keeps them there.

Let's look at fame and success as one value. There must be some part of the need to be successful or part of a successful team (player and caddie) that keeps certain people out there on Tour as a caddie. If they have friends and family who have seen them on the Golf Channel and know their player has had a good result, then they feel great about people congratulating them on a good job or helping their player to achieve a good finish. If the world can see them carrying the bag for a player who is in contention then they have more than their '15 minutes of fame', they are seen as the person beside that great golfer who is helping them to have a great result or even win a Tournament. If you go on *Who Wants to be a Millionaire?* then you may get your 15 seconds of fame, regardless of whether you win $50,000 or get your question wrong. When I was on Millionaire Hot Seat with Eddie McGuire, I made sure that my 15 seconds of fame was a list of my best character impersonations from Get Smart and Hogan's Heroes! Yet as a caddie you are on the screen often if your player is in contention in the final two rounds of a regular or even Major Tournament.

The reasons for why someone chooses to caddie may differ depending on how long you have been doing it for; do you have a dependent wife and children and how old you are? If you are in your 20s and haven't fully decided what career path you want to follow, then you will inevitably have a different focus or set of values than a 50-year-old caddie who has been caddying for 20 years or more. Some of the most famous caddies in the world have started caddying in their 20s and are still caddying in their 40s and 50s – so their five top reasons for being a caddie probably change along the way.

There are some well-known caddies who have made a living out of being a professional caddie and lasted 20 years or more – Pete Bender, Steve Williams, Prodger, Billy, Sponge Waite and Pete Coleman. Have they managed to make a reasonable salary? Have their relationships survived? Have they managed to have a family and see some of their children's milestones – their birth, first tooth, first day at school or winning their Grand Final in a sport?

I'm sure there were guys out there on tour in 1991 and probably still guys out there now who are running away from certain life problems or responsibilities. Some live by the adage of the famous U2 song – 'I Still Haven't Found What I'm Looking For' – they seem to be out there searching for something but still haven't decided or worked out what 'IT' is.

If you can live a life where you are in cheap hotels, making money, drinking with other caddie mates, flying around the country or world, then that existence is an easy 'escapism' for many. Looking back, I wonder whether some of these guys needed a career and money behind them to ensure they could go to Tournaments and try to make a profit each week. What the general public probably don't realise is that whilst you receive a set wage for caddying from Monday to Friday for your player, if you don't make the weekend cut then that is all you get. So, if you had to get flights, accommodation and meals out of your weekly wage then sometimes you either break even or make a few hundred dollars for the week. If your player isn't consistently making the weekend so you can get you 5, 7 or 10% of their winnings, then some weeks you may just break even. It can begin to get difficult out there if money is a problem then your love of the game, your player and the lifestyle can all come into question.

The partying lifestyle and ease of life for some may be a lure – you don't have to go home and cook a meal or look after children. You get off the course by five o'clock and organise to head out with other caddie mates to find a nice place to eat or a bar with some atmosphere to have a few beers and chat up some women. You can have a fling with a local girl you meet at a bar and then next week you are somewhere else – no strings attached. I don't think it has changed much in the past 20 or 30 years – young guys in their 20s or 30s love to have fun, be silly with their mates and party hard. For an Aussie caddie, you get to choose between seeing most of Europe or the United States and get paid to have a free lifestyle. If it gives you the chance to wander and meet people, have fun, experience new cultures and get paid to carry a golf bag around then why wouldn't that appeal to those with a love of sport and a love or understanding of golf.

There were some challenges or lessons I learnt during my time as a caddie in Europe which may be normal or synonymous with life as a backpacker or traveller. In France, my backpack was stolen as I had been in a car that had driven overnight from Spain – now for some backpackers it may have made them warier, living in fear of it happening again or even enough to want to go home to their own country. I think this situation just made me more resilient – yes, I felt anger and frustration at the thieves and the inconvenience of losing some clothing or sentimental items. Yet I just went and bought new clothes and knew that this was the real reason why one takes out travel insurance – so eventually I got some money back for my backpack and clothing.

When you are in the middle of work you can't let this situation effect how you relate to your player or how well you can concentrate on your ability to help your player play well. The caddie community is close for something like that and as you chat to players and caddies on the practice fairway – chat and rumours spread like wildfire and other players and caddies might offer their sympathies – 'sorry to hear about your backpack being stolen', which can help your spirits and ability to 'move on' with things. Something like this probably happens in some sort of way every week to one caddie or another – they might lose their wallet, get into a fight with locals, have their passport stolen etc. Depending on the type of person they are you may or may not hear about it due to shame, embarrassment, pride or not wanting to bother others with their problems. How you deal with it as 'one of those things' or a normal occurrence is how you get on with being a caddie and concentrating on each hole and getting your player to the weekend.

Another challenge for me as a new caddie was to experience and deal with the disappointment of not getting a job. What was more embarrassing or humiliating was that the player I had caddied for in eight Tournaments chose the weirdest, last resort of all caddies as his caddie before I could get to ask him. Maybe I had left the Tour and gone off backpacking when my player needed a regular caddie who would caddie for him for most of the season. Yet you like to think that your efforts equal being valued over someone you see as a desperado, who floated around the Tour without having a permanent golfer and had a reputation for being a real hothead when he wasn't happy with a situation or a person winding him up!

Some may have a go at getting a regular player who is in the top 75 players and guaranteed a start each week. When you receive knock backs for various reasons you may start to doubt your own ability or it can dent your self-esteem and make you ponder whether this lifestyle or career is for you? There are a range of factors and pressures such as having spent money to fly to where the Tournament is, finding a hotel or youth hostel to stay in, so when you don't get a job you know that you've just lost money!

Faced with the prospect of not getting a golfer who can make reasonable money, who you can put up with, or honestly get along well with – you may decide to leave the Tour and go back to a 'real job' or nine-to-five career. If you are from somewhere in Britain and find yourself stuck in Europe struggling to make ends meet or can't get a proper caddie job because you aren't reliable enough, then it can be a lonely place or 'space' to be in. If you are not a resilient or persistent person then it's hard to ride the waves of missed-cut disappointments, waiting for the top ten payday to arrive. Whilst you have a regular player and things are going well or you are making enough cuts to survive or make money then everything is fine. In contrast if you can't find other caddies to room with or share hire cars or even go out to dinner with and have a few quiet beers then life on Tour can be a lonely place.

If you can't get a player or get sacked you may decide to go back to England if you are on the European Tour and get a real job. Similarly, if you love caddying, golf or the lifestyle you may go to the Women's Tour as a way of getting a caddie job. Yet this may be viewed by some as second best, or that you weren't good enough to get a job on the Men's Tour! It's a tough world and other caddies and players can become your harshest critics.

Chapter 5

Earning My Stripes – Rookie Caddie on the European Tour 1991

Craig 'Pazza Popeye' Parry walks off the 9th green at Huntingdale with brother Glen on the bag at the 1984 Australian Masters.

CHAPTER 5

Earning My Stripes – Rookie Caddie on the European Tour 1991

I arrived in Barcelona in February 1991 on my way to a small town in Catalonia called Tarragona for the Spanish Masters. It is interesting looking back on it now – how many people just fly across the world in the hope that they will get a job? For some it was a big risk, taking many out of their comfort zone, yet I was this backpacking adventurer from Australia who was prepared to put myself out there and see what the Universe or fate delivered. It was a case of letting go and 'trust' that led me to fly to Barcelona, get a train to the nearest town to the golf course and find my way to the course and ask players if they needed a caddie. I wasn't thinking – what if I don't get a job, how much has it cost me to get there from London, where am I going to stay, etc. I just trusted that everything would be fine and that I would get some sort of caddie job and make some money to cover my costs.

Since my player missed the cut I may have lost in a monetary sense, yet this was my ticket to future work for other players – I had put myself out there in a life-sense and felt that the universe would provide and things would be great. If I managed to see Barcelona, one of the most historic and vibrant cities in Europe along the way, then that was my bonus – it was a no lose or win–win situation regardless of the result. With a *que sera, sera* attitude I just let life flow over me and generally good things happened – I was in a backpacker, see-the-world mentality so experiencing amazing sights was a bonus; getting a secure caddy job was almost secondary.

I found my way to the course and just turned up hoping a player needed a caddie. Now, an interesting thing about the profession of 'caddying' is that you don't need references or a job interview to get a job, it seems and unwritten law that if you front to a professional golf Tournament and ask a player if he needs a caddie then the player generally assumes that you know something about golf or that you can caddie.

I don't know if the process has tightened up or if players want to know a range of information such as – "Who have you caddied for?" "How long have you been a professional caddie for?" "Did you sack your player or did they sack you?" "Do you play golf off a single figured handicap?" Anyway, I managed to get a bag and I caddied for a rookie Australian player playing his first Tournament on the European Tour – Lucien Tinkler. I carried the bag, did the yardages, gave some advice on putting lines and generally encouraged good shots. Since this was my first Tournament too I wasn't fully prepared for him breaking his Ping Anser copper putter on the bag in anger and having to putt for the rest of round two with driver! Safe to say that this was a rather quiet back nine as he stared the very real prospect of not making the cut, having to drive and putt with the same club. I'm not sure if he made it into many Tournaments that year or went to play the Satellite Tour to get his card or came home but that was the last I saw of Luce that year. As Aussies, we love to give people nicknames for a variety of reasons and this was part of the European Tour that year as caddies from England, Ireland, Scotland, Canada, South Africa, Zimbabwe, Spain, Italy, Argentina and America loved to have nicknames for everyone.

When I mentioned weeks later to another group of caddies that I had caddies for Lucien Tinkler they said – 'Oh, Loosehead Sprinkler'. I am not sure if this was great rhyming slang or referred also to his temper on the course when things weren't going well. In that year, I witnessed many expressions of bad temper from golfers who sometimes acted like spoilt little boys – including breaking clubs, smashing tee markers and breaking them and yelling at the ball to get in the hole!

Week two I travelled across Spain by train to Lisbon and then north to the famous soccer town of Porto. The Tournament just outside Porto, in a seaside town called Povoa De Varzim was the Portuguese Open. Here I secured the bag of a young American rookie from Texas, Brian Nelson, who was there with five or six other young American pros all trying to make their tour card, get experience and win some money. Brian, like many other that season, was sponsored by Ping and had the same white bag that Lucien had, yet a very different personality. Even though he didn't preach the Bible or walk down the fairways like a Praise the Lord Christian, he was a quiet, even-tempered guy who as he was missing the cut just got a bit angry with himself and his stroke play.

Here caddies were like second-class citizens – we were not allowed into the clubhouse, maybe not even into the locker room to get our players clubs. Very different to France, England and Germany where we had access to the clubhouse and sometimes sat with our player or other caddies in there having lunch and a few lagers. Here we missed the cut and I then proceeded to take the longest train trip ever to the next Tournament in Florence in Italy.

The first part of this trip was on a dangerous and rowdy train with Spanish and Portuguese supporters from a soccer match that had just finished in Porto. I was squashed between a lot of foreigners in a six-seat cabin, not keen to leave my seat to go to the toilet for fear of losing my seat, having luggage stolen or being beaten up by the crazed football fans who lined the corridors of my carriage.

A day later with not much sleep we ended up in Hendaye on the French/Spanish border where I found myself on a train with The Munster and his wife, Sully the ex-US Tour caddie from England, and Tattoo Tony the geezer from London. At least these were other caddies who spoke English and The Munster and Sully decided 'Chuckles' was a good nickname for me, as they thought I was funny and always making jokes – or were they sarcastically taking the piss and didn't like my sense of humour? Sully looked like life had been hard – not sure if there had been a wife or wives yet he kept saying – "When I was caddying in the States for Don January we had a few wins and life was good." He loved a bit of the happy weed and I think scotch was his drink of choice – he had a raspy voice that sounded like he had smoked for most of his life and lived life full of celebration. I'm not sure who he caddied for that season but I don't think it was a player that had a good year – that didn't matter to Sully as every year was a good year. If caddying was paying you well then you probably would have flown back to London and then out to Florence or caught a charter flight from Porto or Lisbon to Rome or Florence.

This train through the Riviera to Florence was the way caddies saved money in those days, including British caddies driving their own cars around Europe to save money on flights. It was a competition for off-course bragging rights to see who could find the cheapest two- or three-star hotel, *pensione* or digs as they were referred to in each new city in which you were caddying.

Another interesting observation was that there was no loyalty or patriotism when it came to the sponsorship of a golf Tournament – we had the Volvo Open in Florence, Italy; the Peugeot Spanish Open in Madrid; the Mitsubishi Austrian Open and the Volvo German Open! Volvo the great Swedish car maker was probably the exception that year as the whole Tour was sponsored by them – the Volvo Tour.

Looking back on life on Tour in the 1990s you had to secure a place to stay, usually

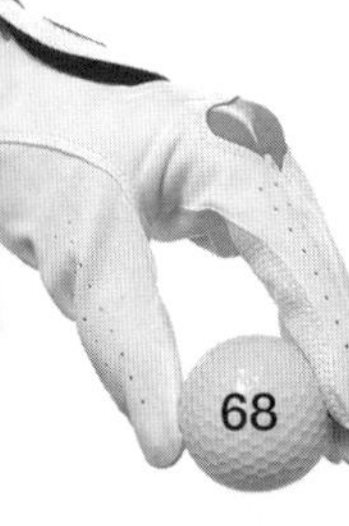

with another caddie, find good cheap places to eat each night, organise something like lunch in a foreign country and work out your laundry so you looked half decent on the course – oh and turn up and concentrate on being a good caddie to assist your player to get his and your best result.

My players missed a few cuts that year which doesn't help pay for flights, meals and accommodation! So, it is in your best interests to do a good job for your player to ensure he plays well, and if he isn't making top 20 finishes or consistently making the cut, then maybe you need to see who else is looking for a new caddie?

Chapter 6

Fun in Florence With Tattoo Tony

Wayne Grady and caddie stand at the back of the 9th green during the 1994 Australian Masters at Huntingdale.

CHAPTER 6

Fun in Florence With Tattoo Tony

When we arrived in Florence I had already paid for Tattoo Tony's train ticket because he said he would pay me back after the Tournament, so we ended up getting a cheap and clean *pensione* in Florence. Now in those days generally you got to the players hotel and jumped on the bus out to the course with your player ready to practise for the day's play. That worked well most weeks and did for the first part of that Tournament.

On the Friday night, Tony and I met up with a few other caddies and decided to go to a popular nightclub which was walking distance to our hotel. We were there until about 3 or 4 am drinking and doing our best to chat up women. When we got back to the *pensione* we asked for a 7 am wakeup call so we could make the bus and get to the course for a 9:40 tee-off time. We went off to our room, which was two single beds beside each other and started snoring. At 7 am when the phone rang with our wakeup call we answered the phone and then rolled over and went back to sleep, having had less than four hours' sleep. At around nine o'clock one of us woke up first and screamed "shit!" when we realised what the time was. We madly threw on clothes and raced outside for a taxi.

We are constantly asking in English/Italian for the driver to go faster as we are seriously dreading the outcome as we find our player out on the course. We finally arrive at the course after a 30-minute trip and ask him how much. This then creates an angry scene as he can't get another job to get him back into central Florence so he demands we pay him for both ways!

We start arguing for a bit then Tony throws some money at him and we race off to find which hole our player is on. When you are out the front of a golf course in a foreign land, I suppose common sense takes over-finding your player with the likely threat that you will be sacked, overrides giving a taxi driver a few more lira!

I catch up to Brian by the 8th hole and approach him cautiously with my tail between my legs. Thankfully Brian is a relaxed Christian type of guy who is actually happy to see me as he has carried his own bag for eight holes. So, I apologise and roughly explain that we slept in and start caddying. For the next three holes, he goes birdie, birdie, birdie and all is forgiven. Now this is amazing as any caddie from that era will tell you that being late for a round would usually mean instant dismissal!

Brian went on to make the cut and he actually finished in 27th position, a great result for a young rookie pro from Texas trying his wares on the European Tour. The irony is that Brian actually sent me a cheque to the flat I was crashing in in London for my 5% of his prize money for that week – I think it was £110 – funny from sacked to getting a percentage of his winnings!

The following week was the Jersey Open in Jersey where I was chasing Tattoo Tony for the money I had lent him for the train ticket– around £100. I was looking for a job and ended up with a celebrity as it was a Pro-Celebrity styled Tournament on the windswept course of La Moye on Jersey. Now every English caddie knew this guy, yet as an Aussie if I hadn't seen him on the Queen's Royal Variety Performance then I didn't know him. He was a well-known

English ventriloquist and comedian named Roger De Corsey; he also happened to be the manager of Ross McFarlane who I would end up caddying for at the next Tournament.

Now it was an interesting week as I had two days on Roger's bag as he played with a Pro and local businessman. If I could remember some of the blue jokes he told them on the way round I couldn't repeat them in this book! Even though I didn't know this unique comic legend from England, I imagine that the jokes I heard were not part of his TV routine where kids might be part of the audience. Not to mention how many times the F-bomb came out after a bad shot – let's say if he had ever walked the fairways with Peter Allis on *Pro Celebrity Golf* in the 1980s it would have screened at nine or ten at night with plenty of beeps!

I managed to catch up with a guy who a friend of mine had met in Kho Samui, Thailand on the way over to London and he was a local who showed me some of the sights. When I got to the airport to fly back to Exeter with other players and caddies, I started chatting to Ross McFarlane asking him where Tattoo Tony was as he owed me some money. Ross was also looking for him as he had asked for next week's pay up front and done a runner! These were the types of dodgy characters that occasionally loitered around the Tour. We also had a guy from Argentina who had an endless supply of cheap leather jackets and when asked if he had anything else, opened the side of the jacket to reveal a good supply of watches – it was like Arfur Daley meets Dell-boy from *Only Fools and Horses*. Shifty stuff off the back of a truck for sale in a place where nobody asked questions – if they could get a real or fake Rolex!

For some reason for the seasoned professional caddies the Rolex was something they bought themselves to say – "I've made it!" or their player gave them when he won it for lowest score or part of a hole-in-one prize. It seemed to me like a status symbol of sorts, maybe it was more the Australasian caddies than the British or European ones – when they earned enough or their player won that they would splurge on a real Rolex!

Anyway, after we flew to Exeter I saw one of the funniest things I have ever seen in an airport – something which can no longer happen thanks to security scares and the way of the world. Justin ('Wood duck' as he liked to call certain caddies as a joke or put down) who was caddying for the Trophy (his nickname due to the shape of his large ears!) aka John Hawksworth decided to play a prank on other caddies as we waited at this tiny airport for our luggage at the carousel.

We were standing at this little airport waiting for our luggage, so he was a bit bored and felt like livening things up for us. So, he slipped onto the baggage carousel when there was no airport staff around and sat there until he came out with the luggage. Some players and caddies had just got to the carousal then as he came out sitting quietly like a suitcase himself, we all laughed our heads off at the practical joke. There were things like that that you could get away with in 1991 that sadly we have become ruled by too many rules and he would be fined or arrested if he tried it today!

The next week I caught the train from London to Plymouth, an amazing town which is where the *Mayflower* left for America in the 1600s. I stayed in a B&B and managed to get lifts out to the course with caddies who hired a car, to get to the practice round or I hitchhiked out there. It was the Benson and Hedges International at St Mellion, a course designed by Jack Nicklaus. I managed to get the bag of an unknown Spanish golfer to me – Jose-Marie Canizares – not quite as world famous as Jose-Maria Olazabal, who was also playing the European Tour that year.

It was an interesting week as other caddies were interested in how much he was paying as certain Spanish golfers had the stereotype of not paying as well as British, American or Australian golfers. I think I got £200 when the going rate was £225–250 that year. We had to put up with fighter jets from a nearby RAF base screaming over our heads in the middle of the round. Also on the Friday we played one of the longest, slowest rounds of golf I have ever been involved in – we won the lottery and got paired with Peter 'Chook' Fowler who for me was agonisingly slow at hitting every shot including his putts. When most players and caddies were ready to pick up the bag and move to the next hole you had to press pause or stop on your body remote control to wait for Chooky to finish!

Chapter 7

Crisis in Cannes

Caddies standing at their players' drives on Hilly Back Nine Par 4 at Ugolino Golf Club, outside Florence. (Volvo Florence Open)

CHAPTER 7

Crisis in Cannes

The following week it was the Madrid Open in Spain and I was looking for a job again as Brian hadn't qualified for this or received a special invitation from the Tour or Sponsors. I was hanging with the other Aussie caddies like Trewie who was caddying for the rookie Pete Lonard, the down to earth bloke from Sydney.

This is where I first hooked up with Ross McFarlane, a young English pro at the time who had been ditched by Tattoo Tony, doing a 'runner' with some of his money. We missed the cut this week and then started an amazing journey across Spain into France.

I had become friends with two caddies from Northern Ireland, Harry who had

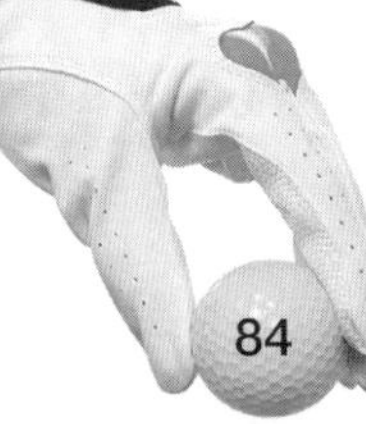

been on Tour a few years, and Sam his mate who had come out this year to try his luck. You couldn't really get two very different people – Harry was a hothead if you got him fired up over something that he saw wasn't right or fair and Sam was more your quiet, happy go lucky type of guy. Harry had driven his Ford Cotsworth Sierra down from Belfast to drive to Tournaments to save on flights. I had heard they were driving to Cannes where the next Tournament was so I asked for a lift and agreed to chip in for my share of petrol.

We arrived in Cannes on the Monday very tired after driving overnight from Madrid. Harry had booked an apartment in town so we were looking for a park so we could organise the keys to it. It seemed a bit funny at the time yet you don't think about it but we indicated to take a parking spot in the street beside the Carlton Ritz, a five-star Hotel in Cannes for the rich and the famous. There was a car which might have been there before us but they let us take the park, which is unusual for aggressive French drivers. We got out of the car and went into the next street to find our accommodation. We were only gone about ten minutes when we returned to the car to get our luggage to find thieves had done a smash and grab, and my backpack was gone and some cash that Harry had in the glovebox. Luckily, they were so quick that my smaller backpack with my camera and other things was left in the back seat. So, we went off to the French Police station to report it and get some paperwork for Insurance claims. I ended up get money back for a new backpack, yet I had borrowed an old Caribee backpack that was my cousin's.

So here we were in Cannes very tired as we had driven most of the night and I had only the clothes I was wearing. The next day I went to the local market and bought some clothes, plus pants, a polo top and runners from the supermarket. That week was a rollercoaster as Ross missed the cut despite having a hole in one that we never saw. He hit onto a raised green and I was looking around for where it finished and finally decided to check the cup and there it was! No prize like a nice car or watch, we couldn't enjoy it and high-five because we didn't see it go in, and then he proceeds to miss the cut.

So, Friday night we went out for Chinese in town, Harry, Sam, myself and a few other caddies. When we went to pay the bill, it had been covered by Vijay Singh who knew we had been robbed and covered the bill and left quietly without telling us – very nice of him and a good finish to a trying week. Kind of difficult to concentrate fully on caddying well when you are in a foreign country that doesn't happily speak English, and you have no clothes and other sentimental things have been stolen from you.

Amazing how a week can change your fortune – the next week was the Spanish Open in Madrid. Ross was in the fourth-last group out on the Sunday with Sam Torrance (I had asked him if he remembered me from the time I caddied for him at the Australian Masters in Melbourne and with some thought he did).

Ross played pretty well and with a par out of the bunker on 18 we finished 4th! I felt the pressure of not making cuts to being in the top ten interesting. Your player becomes a little tenser and I just had to reassure him that clubs were right and to take a smooth swing. As we approached the final green there was a fair gallery in relation to the amount of fans out on the course in total. You feel a real buzz or excitement yourself as you walk down the final fairway with people clapping your player and cameras on you as it was shown every week on Eurosport in those days. Max, a legendary Kiwi caddie who wasn't caddying that week, said to me at the next Tournament, "Hey nice finish in Madrid I saw you on the television!" For a young caddie with not too much experience of being in the top ten, let alone the top five, it was a good feeling that you had helped your player to achieve such a good finish.

That night I was crashing with a couple of other caddies – Hooch from New Zealand, who was caddying for Paul Turner and old Sully, the English journeyman who had caddied on the US Tour for Don January long ago. As I get back to their apartment, they have been watching the golf and having a few cervezas plus some happy weed (hence the nickname – Hooch!) and they are really pleased for me. Sully spat out something like "I knew Ross was gonna have a good finish cos you was on the bag Chuckles."

The strange thing was that I wasn't used to getting 7% of a top ten finish, so when Ross meets me at Heathrow to fly out to fly out to the next Tournament in Milan and hands me £1,000 I didn't know what to do. I was still in 'backpacker mode' and said "What am supposed to do with this in the middle of Heathrow Airport?" thinking someone would rob me. So I quickly shoved it in my money belt which was strapped around my waist and off we went to catch the plane.

They can pay you anything to be sitting in a café near lake Como in the Italian Alps as your base for caddying in a golf

Tournament. Even from the 18th fairway the amazing view behind the clubhouse of the Alps was breathtaking! Ross missed the cut that week so as he flew back to London with other players, I decided to find a bag for the weekend for some more money. Craig Parry – Pazza or Popeye – won the Italian Open and we were all on the same flight back to London. Caddies and players all together – there were plenty of beers drunk and cheers for Pazza as he walked down the plane! These are the times that make the lugging of the bag through all sorts of weather and watching your player hit balls after a round all worth it. It was probably a patriotic theme too, plenty of Aussie golfers – Senior, O'Malley, Clayton, Davis and Riley and caddies from all over Australia and New Zealand all enjoying the party on board as we flew back to London.

Chapter 8

Two Woods and a Taxi – Walking Sideways at Hesketh

Harry and Sam, two caddies from Northern Ireland checking yardages at La Moye Golf Club before the Jersey Open, 1991.

CHAPTER 8

Two Woods and a Taxi – Walking Sideways at Hesketh

After backpacking with a mate from Melbourne through Egypt, Israel and the Greek Islands for June and early July, I returned to the Tour to find a caddie job for the qualifying rounds of the British Open. As I had been travelling for a while I wasn't able to secure the job for Ross but managed to hook up with Brian Nelson at Hesketh for an interesting two-day qualifying round. After day one we were 1-under par and looking good as they only took the top eight I think from each qualifying course and there were two or three courses.

The next day we were hit by the strongest wind I have ever seen on a golf course.

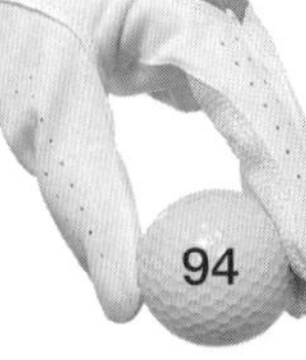

At one par 3 on the front nine players were forced to aim 30–40 metres left of the green to allow for the gale to bring the ball back to the green and when it landed to stay on there! Of the three players in our group only one managed to find the dance floor. We were coming down the back nine and Brian was getting angry with the fierce windy conditions and struggling to keep it together as it seemed like he would miss the cut. He was not the longest hitter but a regulation par 5 that on any normal day pros would reach in two was playing so long he hit driver and Fairway wood and wasn't even close! This was the type of hole that played so long – due to the absolute gale that was howling – that my dad would say it took two woods and a taxi to reach the green!

This was my big chance to go to the big dance, as they call it, for caddies – the Open, where every caddie receives a pair of Footjoy runners to wear. I suppose since you are caddying in Europe the British Open is the biggest event for a caddie, if you made the cut you were guaranteed a fair payday. The consolation for those who didn't make it was to get a job working for the host broadcaster, the BBC, as someone who tells the commentators which club the player is hitting from the fairway.

That week to save money I left my B&B in Southport to go and tent it in the bush not far from the Town. Now people probably wouldn't attempt this these days but I left my gear in a tent in the middle of trees and went without showering for a couple of days to save on accommodation as I had only made £80–100 for caddying for Brian at the qualifying rounds at Hesketh. On the Monday before the Tournament I went to Royal Birkdale for a look at what might have been and chat to a few of the 'lucky' caddies. I took a few photos and bought some souvenirs, like towels, coasters and placemats for myself and my family from the pro shop.

A week later I caught the ferry to Holland and slept in bush near the course the night before and walked in the next day to see who needed a caddie. Ross already had one but I was back on the bag again for the following week in Stockholm for the Scandinavian Masters.

As Sweden was expensive it was an unwritten law that players would pay their caddies £40–50 more for that week as the flight with Air Scandinavia was about £200 alone. Then you had to find cheap digs – two words that don't really exist in Stockholm – cheap and hotel! I'm not sure what some of the other caddies did that week but I went the backpacker option and stayed on the *Gustav af Flint* – which was one of two ships that were used as original styles of accommodation by backpackers. Unfortunately, you can't control drunk people coming in at 12 at night and making lots of noise when you are in a bunk bed dorm of ten people! So, let's say I was rather tired and probably lucky not to sleep in again and miss my tee time.

I managed to find my way each morning to the players' hotel and catch the bus out to the course. Ross missed the cut and I remember spending Friday after my round in the very quiet sponsor marquees with Glen Parry (Craig's brother who was caddying for Mike Clayton) and Pazza's wife. That night I hit the disco with another caddie from Zimbabwe who caddied for Tony Johnstone. This was a bizarre night to say the least!

Firstly, we lined up for about half an hour and chatted up some girls in the line who were locals. When we got in there, one of them happily bought us a beer on her credit card – now I had never seen this in Melbourne or London before. In the '90s we still used cash for lots of things – yet the price of beer in Sweden meant that you needed a credit card otherwise you had to carry £100-200 even to buy a few 'shouts'! For a bloke trying to impress or chat up a girl he doesn't feel great if she buys the first drink! Needless to say, we still managed to stay with these girls all night at the disco. At the end of the night, the nice blonde one who had bought the drinks said she had a boyfriend and that I might hook up with her girlfriend. Anyway, Grant and I went back to their apartment and had a good night!

I flew back to London and got myself ready to catch the train up past Liverpool for the European Pro Celebrity at Hoylake, also known as Royal

Liverpool. This was a links, wind-swept course beside the sea which Peter Thomson had won a British Open at years earlier. Ross played okay but not good enough to make the cut, so I had another Friday finish. The highlight of the weekend was having my Sony Walkman tuned to Radio-1 to hear the Wembley Stadium concert of INXS as I sat in my B&B bedroom on the Saturday night.

The next Tournament was the National Mutual English Open at The Belfry, just outside Birmingham. When I say 'just outside Birmingham' that's what my bus driver thought! I had caught the train up from London, where I was based in a shabby flat in Bayswater with ten other Aussies and Kiwis, and then caught the local bus out of town to as close to the course as I could get. Well I said to the bus driver, "I need to get as close to The

Belfry golf course as I can." Now maybe in the Midlands and North 'close to' means one or two miles away. I had a full backpack, armed with tent and a smaller backpack hanging in front of me. It was average British temperatures for an August day and I set off walking to the course – I kept seeing signs saying The Belfry but the 'short walk' appeared to take for ages – maybe an hour – not my idea of 'close to the course'!

Anyway, I had my tent as caddies had said you can camp on the back of the driving range for the week. So, I set up with about four or five other caddies who were saving money for 'free digs' and we had to shower and change in the players' locker room. Now I grew rather attached to my towel from The Belfry locker room, so I souvenired it and still had it in Australia about ten years later! I'm not sure if 'tent city' exists for some courses on the European Tour these days but it certainly helped to save money, especially if your player missed the cut that week.

Now there was something rather weird or unique about The Belfry – we didn't have to walk down the road and find the local English pub or get permission to have dinner in the clubhouse during the Tournament – there was a pub/disco in the grounds of the course. Such a temptation for young caddies to walk out their tent a few hundred yards and go to get a meal, a few pints of lager and maybe chat up and dance with a girl! Hard life this professional caddie gig! Hard to focus the next day on course with your player when you danced too hard, drank too much or stayed up too late – very unfair to put a disco across the fairway from us!

It was here that on a practice day, the Monday or Tuesday, I was standing on

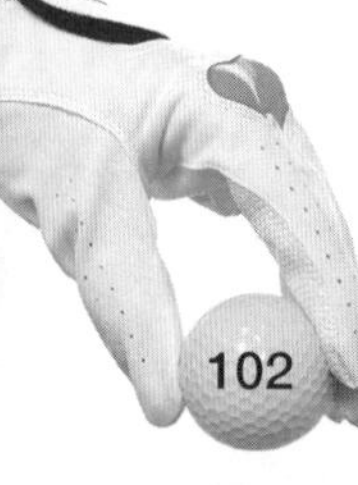

the practice green with players putting and chipping around me and copped a real scare. A young Jesper Parnevik was pitching from a distance to a hole with his caddie standing behind it collecting the balls. I was standing with Ross putting from varying distances when a ball flies past my ear. It scared the shit out of me and as I swung round to see where it had come from – both the caddie and Parnevik were laughing thinking it was a big joke! Had I been caddying for longer or had known either the young, smart Swede or his caddie better, I probably would have said something strong – there was no call of 'fore' to warn me that a ball was close to hitting me!

Another bonus of The Belfry week was that caddies could play on the other 18-hole course after their player had finished for the day. So, I had a round with borrowed clubs as I wasn't game to use Ross' in case something happened to them. It turned into a mini caddies' Tournament as I remember Billy (who at that stage had caddied for Seve Ballesteros and then later Lee Westwood) and maybe three other caddies playing nine holes or one hole with caddies and some players as the gallery on the course used for the Tournament.

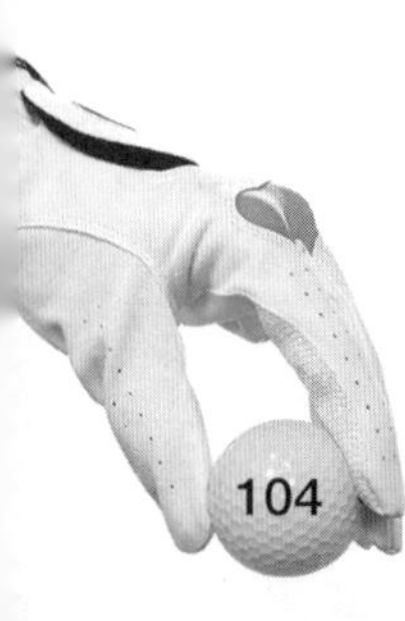

Chapter 9

Get in the Hole!

Australian professional Mike Clayton and caddie, Glen Parry, waiting for players to clear the green at Castelconturbia Golf Club outside Milan with a breathtaking view of the Italian Alps behind the impressive clubhouse.

CHAPTER 9

Get in the Hole!

The following week was the German Open in Dusseldorf and I caught a charter flight from London for about £90. Again, the experienced caddies said you could camp again, so some of the same caddies from The Belfry pitched their tents out beside the second course. We would borrow our player's clubs – 9-iron and wedge and play a few holes each night. Otherwise we caught the local bus into town to find a place to eat and a pub to drink at. It was here that I heard one for the strangest accents I have ever heard – a German barmaid had learnt English from someone Irish and had a German-Irish English accent-weird! I had heard Swedes with American accents due to television or their language teacher, yet this took the cake.

Now this was a really good week for me, I stayed on the course for free and Ross made the cut and shot up the leader board on the last day, shooting 66. He holed a few snakes which saw me taking out the flagstick and helping the ball into the hole with some - 'get in the hole' whilst slamming my hand down as it dropped in. Wow, there is no better feeling than enthusiastically helping the ball into the hole with an animated action – especially when it does actually drop in for a monster birdie putt. Also, you never knew what next week held so any good finish was a welcome bonus as it meant a good payday!

On the par 3 on the front nine he holed a 40-foot putt with a big right to left swing – which was mainly him as he didn't ask much advice on the line of putts. Then on the final hole he dropped in a 20-foot birdie to finish with a 66 and leap up the leader board from 30th to equal 8th with Rodger Davis from Australia.

We then sat on a table with other players and caddies and ate lunch and had a few pints watching the leader board. Now this week there was a Rolex watch for the lowest round of the Tournament, so Ross made me go down to the outside leader board to see if anyone had had a 66, and what their back nine was like as he could still win the watch on a countback. We thought we had the watch secured as the last few groups finished their rounds. Now I don't know what happens to that sort of prize – would the player give it to the caddie or was he obliged to pay him 5% of its worth as his cut or bonus?

Ross had the watch on his wrist until Paul Broadhurst shot 65 to win the Tournament by one shot and steal the Rolex from Ross. Later at the airport Broady, who was a nice guy and mates with Ross said "Sorry about taking the Rolex off you."

During the Tournament, I had the luxury of using a new brand of mobile phone that was being promoted at the advertising tent by a German phone company. They let me ring anyone anywhere in the world so I called the shabby flat in London to ask them if I was still going on my Contiki Tour of Russia and Scandinavia as there had been political unrest, a minor coup and tanks in the streets of Moscow shooting at people demonstrating. They said it was still on yet I found out later that the Tour before us had been cancelled.

So, when I got back to London I confirmed with my London backpackers travel agent that we were still going on the tour despite the problems in Russia. On the trip, we had a tour theme song that got played each morning as we got on the bus to go and visit each city and its sights – ours was 'Winds of Change' by The Scorpions which had an eerie truth to it as it was about the Russian revolution and certain Moscow famous historical landmarks are mentioned. Knowing that there had been a minor revolution, political unrest and people killed in the streets of Moscow made our trip even more real. Being on a tourist bus we were seriously searched both entering and leaving Russia – on the way out to the Polish border we jumped the three-day queue of cars, vans and buses yet they still checked our bus thoroughly to ensure we weren't hiding any boxes of cheap vodka to take to the 'West'!

I then went off seeing the world again and took a Contiki tour of Russia and Scandinavia – just weeks after a mini-revolution and protests in the streets of Moscow.

Chapter 10

Spain's Lee Trevino Lookalike?

Top ten players at the Canon Shootout at Wentworth Golf Club in Surrey at the Volvo British PGA Championship (Olazabal, Torrance, Faldo, Richardson, Ballesteros, Langer, Lyle, Rafferty and Woosnam)

CHAPTER 10

Spain's Lee Trevino Lookalike?

At the end of my Russia-Scandi tour I left it in Berlin and went back to find a caddie job at the Austrian Open just outside of Salzburg. I managed to catch up with big Ronald from South Africa and shared a local home he had rented with a few other caddies. It was walking distance to the course.

Here I managed to get the bag of a Spanish pro called Juan Quiros, who initially to me was a small Spanish version of the Tex Mex – Lee Trevino. Now I had the privilege as a teenager caddie at Metropolitan of standing in the foyer to the Members locker room when Trevino was out for the Vic Open in 1981 and listening as he had a crowd of 20 people in stitches as he told story after story and joke upon joke for 30 minutes straight!

Maybe not quite as funny, but that's who he reminded me of. He couldn't tell jokes and stories like Trevino but he had a sense of humour that his fellow Spaniards understood. Now as every caddie has nicknames for most people I get asked from other caddies, "Oh you're caddying for Queerarse are you?" He has an average round on the Thursday and needed to shoot something good on Friday to make the cut. Now it was here that I was pretty proud of my ability as a caddie to call the right club for a guy I had just started caddying for, as every player had slightly different distances they can hit the ball for each club.

We were heading down the 8th hole and he has an approach to the green, so I work out and tell him the yardage – he thinks 9-iron, I stick with 8-iron. He hits his shot and is on the green but short – a club short by all concerns. The next hole is a par 3 and he asks me the yardage and what club I think, this time it's similar yet into the wind, so I say 8-iron and he decides to go with 9-iron and it just makes the front edge of the green. Now for some players not playing well this is the time the caddie cops it, but since I was right he can't say anything. As we leave the tee, I just look over at the other caddie in my group and say, "What else can I do?" – as if to say I have given him two good reads in a row and he won't listen to me cos I'm just a caddie in Spanish eyes.

Later, as it appears obvious that we are going to miss the cut he starts to get angry at the ball every time he misses a close putt – yelling at the ball or the green as if it is their fault his putt didn't drop. Generally, when you are caddying for a hot-headed player who is about to miss the cut, it isn't a great idea to be seen laughing at how funny it might seem as he blames everything else for his poor play. I am looking at him putt, miss and curse whilst the smartarse English caddie behind him is looking at me laughing his head off quietly in the background. So, I don't know where to look in case I start laughing and he sees me then steam will really come out of his ears and he will let fly at me.

So, Juan pays me my wage and he is playing then next week so I am on the bag for another week – the Mercedes German Masters in Stuttgart. Here the players have a special bus tour of the Hugo Boss factory where they manage to get suits and shirts for a good price or even get sized up by Tailors for a personal fitting suit.

Great for us jealous caddies who must listen to their stories about how many suits, shirts and pants they managed to get custom-fitted for a good price whilst on the practice range and putting green.

Mercedes German Masters I am caddying for Juan Quiros again and he has an average round on the Friday and we miss the cut again. He pays me and I decide to go to the Oktoberfest to get pissed with all the other Aussie backpackers and it just happens to be the next Tournament. I get to the driving range on the Monday and suss out any jobs as it is late in the season, and to my disgust Ross has taken on the mumbling Italian caddie who has had more bags that I've had hot dinners – you know for most players the last resort caddie. So, by the start of the Tournament I have no job yet manage to camp in my Tent on the course for free.

On the Wednesday night, I agree to go out with Cameron from Canada to a bar he knows as he has a German girlfriend who he stays with when he is in Munich. Now this would have to be one of the weirdest nights out in my life! We get to this bar and I haven't eaten dinner and we start drinking and that's where my memory ends for that evening! Supposedly, according to Cam, I was very drunk and embarrassing to people around me in the bar, especially creepy to some women. All I can remember was going to the toilet to throw up and then I made a wise choice and decided to leave there.

Luckily, I have a pretty good sense of direction, yet this was Munich at night – a foreign city to me! and I was extremely drunk – miraculously I managed to walk and stumble three miles to the players' hotel. Here the porters feel sorry for me and allow me to crash on the couch in a hidden part of the hotel lobby at about 2 am and then wake me up to catch the player courtesy car out to the course in the morning. At the course, I stagger back to my Tent and crash for the extra four or five hours of sleep needed to help my hangover. Definitely not the best night of my life as it feels embarrassing and almost disturbing to not be in control and not be able to remember half the night. Maybe on some level I was just drowning my sorrows as it was my last Tournament of the year and I had no caddie job.

On the Friday things improve, as a young American Ronald Stelton asks me to caddie for him over the weekend. He plays okay on Saturday and draws the prize playing partner on the Sunday of Bernhard Langer. Now golf isn't huge in Germany, yet when there is any gallery you know most of it will be watching their countrymen, the famous, world-renowned Bernhard Langer. Now he is a serious and methodical golfer who really concentrates on his golf, whilst his caddie, the Englishman Pete Coleman is a really nice guy who can have a joke at the right time. I am thinking what a life this caddying one moment no job and so drunk I can't remember half the night and what happened next thing I am caddying beside one of the greats in front of his home country gallery!

This was the last Tournament of the year so on the Sunday night I asked the German barmaid if she wanted to go out for a drink. She took me to her local bar and then back to her place. The next day she dropped me back at the course so I could pack up my tent. That was where my European Tour ended as I didn't have a player in the top 50 who made it to the Volvo Masters at Valderamma, where every caddie was assured of a percentage as there was no cut just finishing positions.

Chapter 11

In the Rough

Practice round at Royal Birkdale for the British Open which was won by Australian Ian Baker Finch.

CHAPTER 11

In the Rough

It is an amazing story that the 17-year-old from New Zealand who caddied for Peter Thomson at Parapamau in the New Zealand Open would go onto caddie for some of the greatest golfers to ever play the game. He was for years the highest paid sportsman in New Zealand, ahead of its cricketers, basketballers and even pro golfers.

In my early days as a caddie at the Australian Masters at Huntingdale I looked up to Steve Williams or the 'Big Cat' (as he was nicknamed then) as a somewhat legend among caddies, as he carried the bag for Greg Norman, with his long hair and big handlebar moustache. We all knew he was a low handicap golfer who marched along the fairways with a real purpose and confidence beyond his years. Funnily enough I was probably 15 and he was 20 yet he confidently prowled and marched up those fairways like a black panther – with his long hair, moustache and strong body – it was like he'd been doing it for years!

In those days, the Masters was held in February and was the last Tournament on the Australasian Tour. We used to have a caddie's Tournament at Huntingdale on the Monday following the Tournament and Steve would usually win it or Phil Wright who caddied for Ian Baker-Finch in those days was one of his rivals.

Steve had a persona that oozed confidence and a 'don't mess with me' attitude as a caddie. If you took a photo whilst his player was hitting a shot you were in danger of having your camera taken, possibly shoved down your throat or he would verbally attack you so you would never do that again. All this and he was still only 20 years old.

Mick Middlemo joined the list of caddies who have sacked or been sacked by Robert Allenby over his career to 30 plus. More recently after a season of abuse when Allenby allegedly called him a 'fat ****' Mick had had enough and put down the bag and walked off the course. If you're a new caddie to the Tour and Allenby is your only bag you'd probably go without.

If we complain about how our player treated us, then we've got nothing to worry about compared to what Mick Middlemo must have endured. If a player is getting angry at you then it might mean that their golf game is going down the toilet and they choose to take it out on the easiest target – the caddie. Now Jerry Lewis may have been clumsy and noisy in *The Caddie* but I don't think Dean Martin felt the need to abuse him or put him down or make cracks about his weight.

One question to ask is "Is it worth $2,000 a week on the US Tour if your player constantly misses the cut and blames or abuses you for his mistakes?" Ultimately, he is the one holding the club – right or wrong club or yardage– a bad shot is the player's responsibility not the caddie's. If there is a personality clash or if you're not enjoying your time on the bag, then maybe it's time for a new player. Believe it or not caddies have sacked their player before – it may appear to some that the player is always in control of this but no, if the caddie has had enough for whatever reason and they have the mental strength they tell the player that the relationship isn't working – just like any couple. Unfortunately, it has happened before to Robert

Allenby from the seasoned caddie from New Zealand, Mike 'Sponge' Waite at St Andrews.

If players get a reputation for not being nice to a caddie, then certain caddies will steer clear of them even if they are the last bag going! Your role is to carry the bag, read the lines of putts, ensure yardages are added up correctly and to say the right things at the right time to keep your player on track during a round. If you are lazy or a 'yes' person, then there's a fair chance you won't stay with that player for too long. I have seen some very spoilt little brats or big babies out there on Tour – some who are so nervous and superstitious that if you don't have the right numbered balls dotted in the bag when they need a new one that can cause a tantrum or trauma, of which you bear the brunt.

Certain European Tour winners who are well known have had their share of

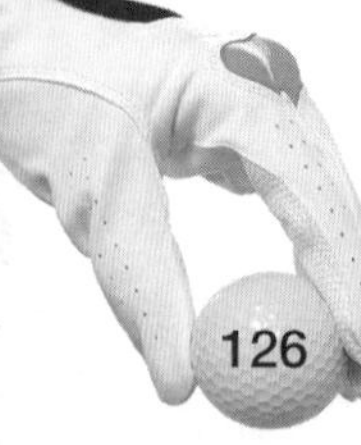

club breaking or tee marker smashing after a bad hole or missing a crucial putt. The threat of missing the cut on the Friday of a Tournament can cause irrational behaviour in many golfers – whether it's their 5th Tournament or their 50th. A certain Spanish golfer who was in danger of missing the cut one day was screaming at the ball after missing many crucial short putts – a trait displayed by many a local club golfer over the years.

It is difficult to know what to say to your player if he is in the middle of horror patch of holes. In caddie lingo, it is called 'having a mare', which basically means your player is about to miss the cut or going from bad hole to bad hole and you as part of the team naturally feel it too. Mentally the player who isn't able to correct their poor shots can create a vicious circle for themselves, whereby they can't recover from one bad hole and the ripple effect means that are 3 or 4 over par in the space of a few holes. As the caddie, you must know what and how to say something that points them in a positive direction in a caring calm manner.

'Okay refocus now it's gone and this is a new hole' is one strategy for helping your player out of a bad run mid or late round. It also depends on the gravity of the situation, e.g. steadying the ship in the second round to avoid missing the cut can be very different to what you might say mid round in a regular Tournament when you might be slipping from 20th to 25th at the end of the fourth round.

'Smooth swing' is a generic statement uttered by many caddies implying that you need to keep your rhythm and not try to hit the cover off the ball to get it further or because you are angry with whatever happened on the previous hole. Finding that good shot or putt that allows you to break the tension is always helpful and ensuring that your body language doesn't show your player that you have given up on them. For many Pro golfers, the caddie is part of the team and the bond can be so strong that you have a strong influence on the ability of your player to pull themselves out of any slump in a round.

If you get frustrated with your player's attitude or inability to hit a positive stroke and get back on that 'birdie train' then fair chance they will see and feel that you have lost confidence in them and the down spiral continues. Sports psychologists can be extremely important in professional golf as many believe 80–90% of good play is above the shoulders. If you look at players on the driving range they can all hit the ball 'pure', yet the difference between finishing top ten regularly and just making the cut to finish 50th every week is in the mind – belief is a wonderful thing.

If a golfer has the ‘yips’ like Ernie Els displayed at the first hole of the 2016 Masters, then it probably doesn’t matter if he uses a broomstick putter or a regular putter. Adam Scott has shown his ability to transfer back to a traditional putter after winning the Masters with a broomstick version in 2013, he started 2016 with two wins on the US PGA Tour, proving that he has the right belief about putting the ball in the hole regardless of what type of putter he is holding.

In my opinion the difference between a good caddie and a great caddie is their ability to guide their player with club selection, trusting their own judgement and sticking with it at the right times and being able to say the right thing to help their player hold the lead or take the lead to win an important Tournament. If you understand your player and can say the right thing in a crucial stage of a Tournament, then you feel confident yourself in your ability to help him by choosing your words carefully to get the best finish possible for them.

Chapter 12

The 19th Hole – A Caddie's Life

Me standing on the 18th tee at St Andrew's, considered the 'Mecca' for golfer's worldwide!

CHAPTER 12

The 19th Hole – A Caddie's Life

So, what are the life lessons for me and other caddies from all the range of emotions and experiences that occur over one or ten seasons as a caddie? There must be something in this profession that makes it enjoyable and sustainable for many men between 20 and 40? Have they created a life where they feel wanted, appreciated or loved by their player or some golf fans? It needs to be something strong or fulfilling to motivate them to remain on Tour where life is living out of a suitcase and flying or travelling from town to town, living in a new Hotel each week.

For me it was a great free lifestyle for that year, yet certain secure aspects of life

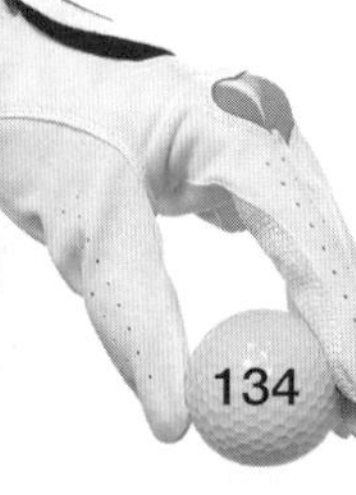

that I have now and cherish, were not part of the nomadic lifestyle of a caddie. It was definitely a 'rockstar existence' which didn't involve or include coming home to your wife and children. Having worked in a regular job as a teacher for over twenty years, caddying was a backpacking type of lifestyle where your biggest worry was usually what restaurant or bar are we going to tonight?

This was an incredible year and ride of a lifestyle where I can remember it now and all the emotions and joy of that whole experience creates a rush to my heart that is unbelievable. If therapists have asked me to picture a time in your life when you had joy, peace and freedom than this would be it. If I could anchor all of the trials and tribulations/challenges of my daily life now with the 'feelings' around that time as a caddie then I would constantly be able to walk around with a smile on my face all day! Who wouldn't love to hold such a feeling of joy and freedom coupled with some abundance of income from a player who made the cut and had a top 20 finish.

Maybe that is what keeps some people as a professional caddie for 20 or 30 years – or most of their life. Now Pete Coleman appeared to be one of those –did he have a family, did he love life on the Tour or did he enjoy that special relationship with a very successful player who made enough prize money to allow the caddie to live a good life?

Obviously, there was a love of golf and being with a player who was making enough money to give him a particular lifestyle too. Pete managed to have a wife who needs to be patient and understanding of the life where he could be in Europe or America for a Tournament for 30-40 weeks of the year.

Do caddies now need to have a partner who is happy to only see them on Sunday nights for most of the year? In 1991, as mentioned, The Munster had his wife on tour with him and she caddied for other players occasionally. Now this was a very unusual set-up which must have worked for them. Relationships either start before the caddie has decided to go on Tour – seen by their partner as an amazing opportunity – or after the caddie has been on Tour for a while where the partner understands what life can be like and duly accepts that situation.

Do we as caddies run on the adrenalin of a good finish? Is it the money or the thrill of carrying a bag beside a huge gallery where many of them are cheering on your player to finish well or win? I believe that we arrive at a point by creating that moment or special feeling in some way. If we are going through the motions in life or believe that we have a player who will have average results, then that is what will appear in our lives. In some respects, we are perpetuating a self-fulfilling prophecy by our values, goals and beliefs – i.e. if we strongly believe our player or even ourselves as caddies are capable or deserving of a top five finish or to win a Tournament, then that is what we will attract. Conversely if we are struggling to get a regular player, make cuts or have a player who makes sufficient money to give us a reasonable income then that is what you believe is possible and will continue to attract and receive in your life.

This may appear strange and weird to many caddies and people in general yet that can be because you are not stopping to view life experiences and situations from this perspective. The reasons for being a caddie in the first place may override any self-doubt about whether this unreal, unique lifestyle is what you choose for your life.

Some like Pat Janssen have caddied for a few years then gone onto be a player manager with the background of understanding what players are going through from week to week.

That amazing year in Europe or helping Norman make his first video were some of the best experience of my life – a time of freedom, joy and great fun. Not everyone gets to live the dream – going around the world carrying a golf bag – especially if it's something you love! It's a rather unique position – you get to make money without the real pressure of hitting the great golf shot to finish well or win a Tournament.

Can this emotion lead to creating a perfect life – caddying in front of big crowds, making good money and travelling the world in a free, partying lifestyle – can you take this feeling into a steady life with a steady job and a family? If you can create and maintain this magic 'feeling' in a 9-to-5 lifestyle, then you live as if you are coming off the 18th green with a top ten finish for your player all the time!

My advice to any guy in their 20s who loves golf, plays it and understands it – go forth young man, see the world, have a party and then decide if you want this for a lifelong career or take the experience and go back to a nine-to-five job with security and regular pay and hours. If family and a stable, secure relationship is what you're after, then living out of a suitcase week after week probably won't deliver this lifestyle or be for you long term. You don't really get paid extra if your player is a perfectionist who feels the need to hit some more practice balls after his round – and you have to stay there and watch, praise, reassure him and listen to him as he tries to cure his mistakes from the round!

This was an amazing period in my life, similar to the boys from *Top Gear* – I was paid to do something that I loved! Walking around some of the best golf courses in the world, in front of big galleries of golf fans– and getting paid for it! I was seeing the world as hopped from one European Country to another, experiencing different cultures and doing my best to help my player achieve his best.

Life as a professional caddie may be different now to how things were back in 1991, but the same ideals and values are needed by caddies today. Whether they perceive this 'career' as an interim five-year plan or a lifelong occupation, they certainly experience a 'high' in this international nomadic existence.

Looking back on this magical feeling or emotion and being able to recapture this or feel this way in other careers, situations or experiences in my life has been the challenge. If I could bottle that 'feeling' and find that joyous, relaxed and free feeling daily then life would be brilliant. We get so caught up in life, family, career and day to day pressures that it is difficult to retain that feeling.

This was an amazing time and experience in my life and one I am truly grateful that I chose to create and enjoy my life as a tour caddie!

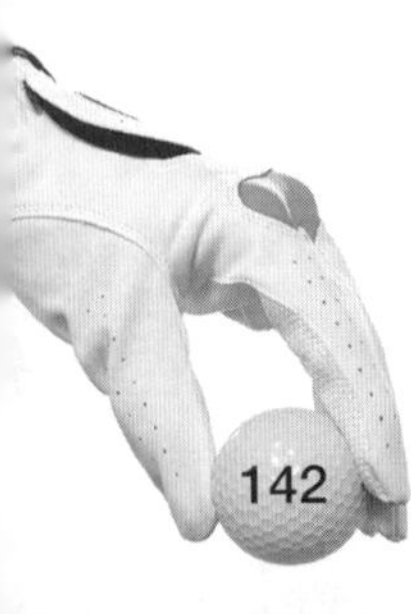

ABOUT THE AUTHOR

David Kight

Author, Educator
and professional Sports Manager

David is an author, educator, and highly esteemed sports management professional.

A lifelong sports enthusiast, at the age of 15, David caddied for Greg Norman during the filming of the golf legend's first golf video.

While a student, David excelled in cricket, football and golf.

After graduating from La Trobe University with a degree in education, David went on to complete his Master's degree in sports management from Deakin University.

Throughout his career, David has worked with many sports organisations, including Racing Victoria, Cricket Victoria, Tennis Victoria and Golf Victoria. He has also had the pleasure of working with Australian Rules football players Shane Crawford and Luke Hodge, as well as comedian Peter Helliar.

He is also a man with diversified interests. David is a talented photographer who has won awards for the striking images he has captured. Additionally, he has won awards for his comedic impersonations.

David's professional associations include membership in the Victorian Institute of Teaching and the Australian Council for Health, Physical Education and Recreation.

An avid traveller, he has travelled and worked in Russia, Finland, Sweden, Denmark, the Greek Islands, Egypt, Ireland, Scotland, the United States of America, Thailand and most of Europe.

David Kight is the author of *Revelations of a Tour Caddie* and lives in Victoria, Australia with his wife and two children.